GLADIATORS

DON'T
FORGET
TO ENTER THE
GREAT
COMPETITION

£5.50

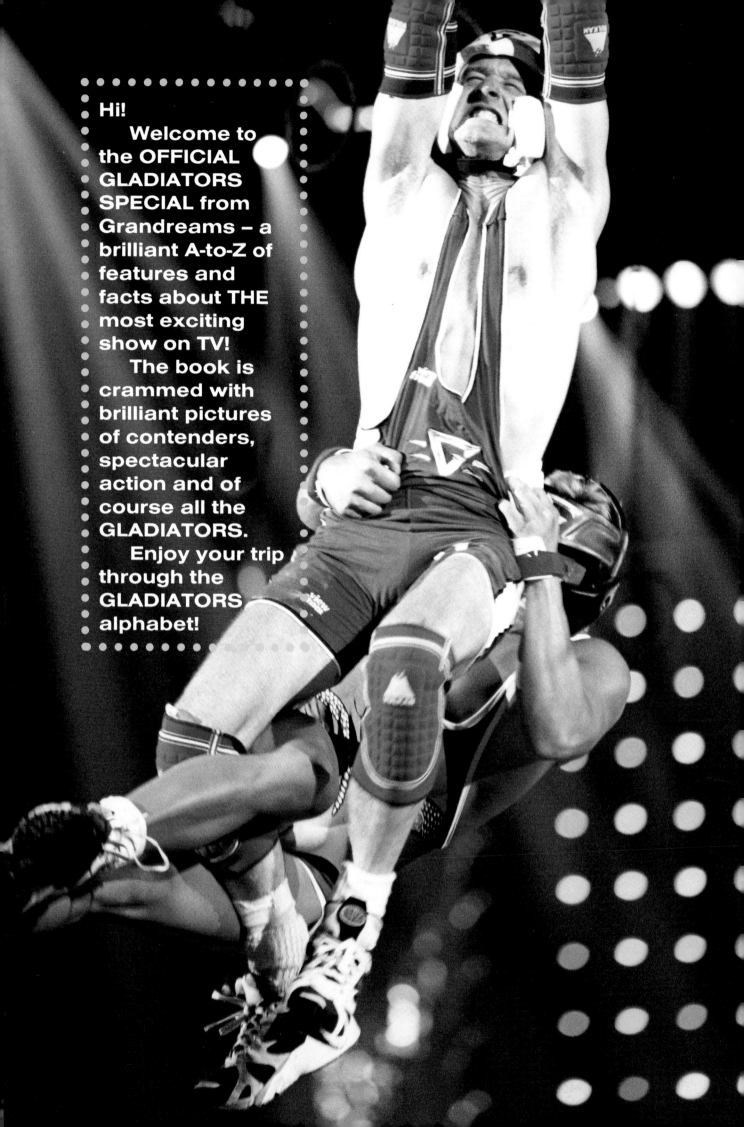

Hi!
Welcome to the OFFICIAL GLADIATORS SPECIAL from Grandreams – a brilliant A-to-Z of features and facts about THE most exciting show on TV!
The book is crammed with brilliant pictures of contenders, spectacular action and of course all the GLADIATORS.
Enjoy your trip through the GLADIATORS alphabet!

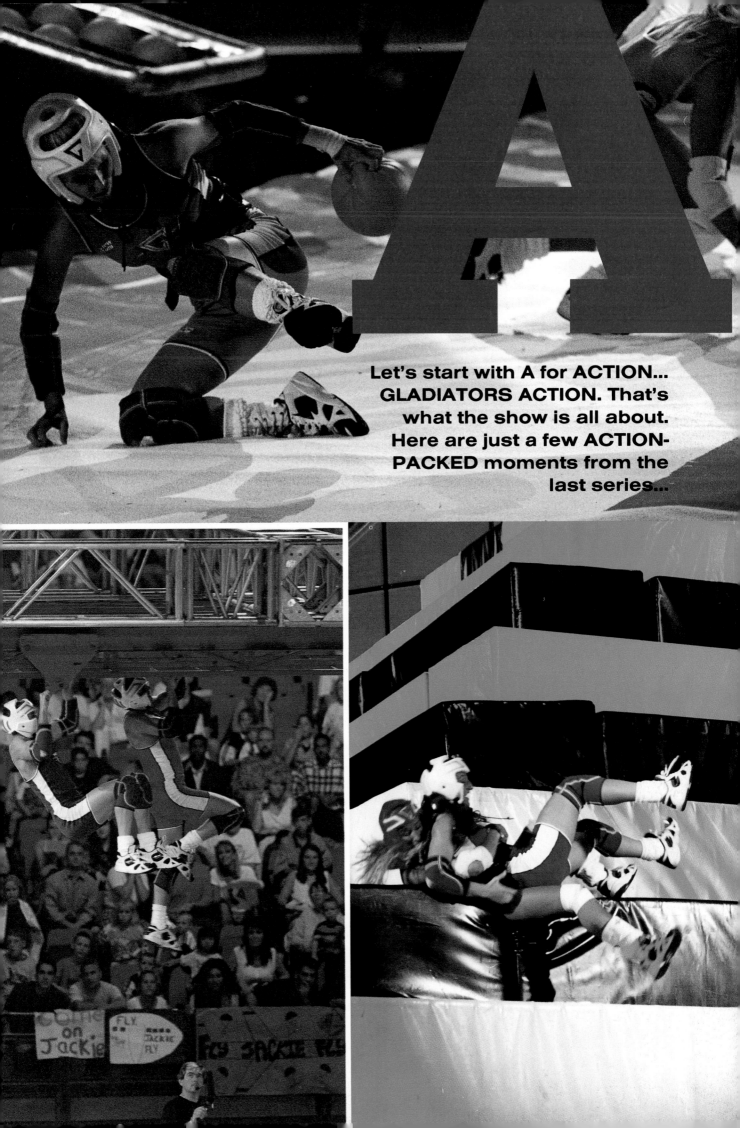

A

Let's start with A for ACTION... GLADIATORS ACTION. That's what the show is all about. Here are just a few ACTION-PACKED moments from the last series...

Amazing Amazon was already a famous lady in her own right before she joined Gladiators. As Sharron Davies MBE she was the proud possessor of two Commonwealth Games gold medals, had competed in no less than three Olympic Games – and she had over 200 British records to her name.

On retiring from competitive swimming in 1995 she became involved with Gladiators via her husband Derek Redmond, the show's trainer and timekeeper. "I was holding a stopwatch in the try-outs because they were short handed," she recalls. "They kept saying 'this is silly why don't you do it!?!'"

The offer was too tempting to refuse and the famous swimmer quickly joined the Gladiators. The next step was the choosing of a suitable Gladiator name. "LWT were keen for it to be something a bit 'watery' because of my swimming, but they also wanted something tough and warrior-like, to go with the image of the show. 'Amazon' seemed to do both."

AMAZON

Amazon found that becoming a Gladiator was a good way to stay competitive without having to train six hours a day as she had done as a swimmer. "Gladiators is recorded in the summer and, though I train every day by habit it now tends to build up much more towards the summer."

She was an instant hit and she discovered that she being a Gladiator is just as tough as competitive swimming. "Gladiators is 'Sports Theatre', it's very different from Olympic Sports. It's very physical and you get knocked about, but it's great fun. Just as much enthusiasm and effort goes into it as in a big swimming competition - it's 100% all the time. And I thoroughly enjoy being part of the team – everyone backs everyone else up."

Amazon's favourite event is Powerball. "...because it's tough and needs goods teamwork."

And her least liked event? "Tilt and Whiplash are very difficult for us to win - they're both very 'anti-Gladiators'. If you don't start on an even keel then you are definitely at a disadvantage. With the men it's not so difficult because they've usually got a huge weight advantage, but it is difficult for the women because we're usually evenly matched with the contenders."

Amazon's first season as a Gladiator was cut short when she received a knee injury during a particularly hectic bout of Pyramid. But now she's back and raring to go again. "I've really enjoyed it," she says. "Everyone has been great and I'm really looking forward to my second series."

► AMAZON FACTS ◄

BIRTHDATE:
1 NOVEMBER 1962

BIRTHPLACE:
PLYMOUTH

STARSIGN:
SCORPIO

HEIGHT:)
180CM (5' 11"

WEIGHT:
67KG (10ST 7LBS)

STATS:
97-66-91CM (38-26-36 INS)

PRESENT HOME:
THE COTSWOLDS

FAVOURITE MUSIC:
TINA TURNER, LUTHER VANDROSS

FAVOURITE ACTORS:
ARNOLD SCHWARZENEGGER,
SYLVESTER STALLONE

FAVOURITE TV SHOWS:
ROSEANNE, FRENCH & SAUNDERS

John Anderson, the Gladiators' referee and timekeeper, is the man who all Gladiators bow to. He's not scared of any of them, no matter how big and strong they are!

Even Wolf at his worst has to cower when John issues a warning or a reprimand!

Dressed in his black & white stripes and armed with whistle, stopwatch and rulebook, the referee has the final word on any disputes that may arise in any event. Sometimes he refers to video evidence to make a judgement.

Make no mistake, John Anderson's word is Law!

John is assisted by official timekeeper Derek Redmond.

A NDERSON

Caged inside 2m (7ft) diameter Atlasphere, two Contenders head for the scoring pods, while two Gladiators – also in 'spheres – attempt to stop them in their tracks! If an Atlasphere hits the sensor in a pod, a plume of CO_2 is released. Three points are awarded for each successful score.

A TLASPHERES

BIRMINGHAM

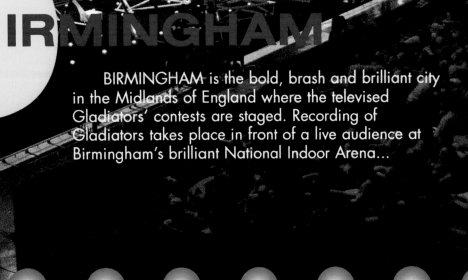

BIRMINGHAM is the bold, brash and brilliant city in the Midlands of England where the televised Gladiators' contests are staged. Recording of Gladiators takes place in front of a live audience at Birmingham's brilliant National Indoor Arena...

BEHIND THE SCENES

Producing the fifteen episodes of Gladiators that make up a series is like a military operation for producer Ken Warwick and his team.

• During the two weeks it take to set up all the staging and lighting at the National Indoor Arena, the Gladiators will be practising all the events

• Twelve cameras are used in the recording
• Reserve contenders are always on stand-by in case of accidents
• Two Gladiators shows are recorded in a day
• Each hour long show takes an average of four hours to record
• Editing a single show takes two days

™

COBRA

Cobra always makes quite an entrance with his sensational high kicks and his bouncy personality. And the youngsters just love him because he's a natural born comic who is always clowning around.

Cobra has two ginger cats and a black-and-white one – and they all keep an eye on his Alsatian called 'Rebel'.

But in the arena he is as lethal as the snake that gives him his name. He is combative and competitive and just hates to be beaten.

Cobra's favourite Gladiators event is Hang Tough, but he enjoys all the others too – except perhaps one – The Wall– which he reckons is a bit too hard on the biceps and tendons!

Did you know that Cobra's Gladiators career began when he wrote in and applied to be a contender, because he had been a great fan of American Gladiators? But when the show's producers saw his blond hair and tanned body they decided he should be a Gladiator – and so Cobra was created!

▶ COBRA FACTS ◀

BIRTHDATE:
29 OCTOBER 1963

BIRTHPLACE:
DARTFORD

STARSIGN:
SCORPIO

HEIGHT:
183CM (6')

WEIGHT:
95KG (15ST)

STATS:
CHEST 122CM (48") WAIST 81CM (32")
THIGHS 66CM (26") ARMS 47CM (18.5")

"Contenders ready..."
When a contender hears those two words pronounced by referee John Anderson they know they have made it to the big time. They know that all the effort has been worthwhile.

CONTENDERS

Contenders for the current series first applied at the beginning of the year, along with some 25-30,000 other hopefuls. When all the application forms were sorted and sifted by the Gladiators' computer, more than a third of the applicants were invited to take part in try-outs all over Britain. At the try-outs they had to pass a series of tests, with short rest periods in between. The tests are as follows:

- **Run 800m on treadmill (men in 2 mins, women in 3 mins)**
- **Pull-ups on Rig. Hold for 5 secs (men 10 times, women 5 times)**
- **Climb along an overhead 4.5m monkey ladder, then climb and descend rope (men climb rope twice, women once)**

Contenders successfully completing those tests progress to a Pugil Stick fight with another contender to determine levels of aggression. Contenders alternately attack and defend in two 30 seconds bouts with a 30 seconds rest in between. Then both attack for 30 seconds. The object of this test is to judge not only if a potential contender can wield a Pugil Stick correctly, but also to see if they react over-aggressively in a fight situation. Contenders have to be tolerant.

Finally comes a brief interview on camera, in which the applicant's personality is assessed. Potential contenders must be bright and positive and certainly not camera shy!

From the try-outs 50 probable contenders are selected. From these the final 32 – 16 men, 16 women – are chosen.

All they have to do after that, is battle it out with those awesome Gladiators!

DANGER ZONE

A super event in which the Contender has one minute in which to avoid tennis balls fired at him or her by a Gladiator marksman!

At the same time the Contender has to negotiate a way to four 'safe stations' which they have to defuse within ten seconds and fire a weapon at the target above the Gladiator. Once through the four stations it's into the perspex tube to hit a target beneath the Gladiator!

One point is earned for each station reached. Ten points awarded for hitting the target above the Gladiator. Five points for hitting the target beneath the Gladiator.

DIET

Gladiators love their food, but obviously they have to eat a sensible diet, especially during the recording of the show. Basically they eat for health, strength, stamina and performance. This means lots of pasta, bread, rice, white meat, fish and fruit – and they drink plenty of water!

Nightshade says she eats a very sensible diet. "And I love West Indian and Indian food with lots of spices. Luckily I find many healthy dishes within those cuisines. The secret is to eat in moderation."

Amazon says that during the recording of Gladiators she is not very good with food. "I've always been that way – when I'm nervous food is the the last thing on my mind. I have to make sure that I've got a bar of chocolate in my bag - otherwise I'll go for hours without eating. But normally I'm a very sensible eater."

DUEL

Standing atop 1.1m (4 ft) diameter platforms Contender and Gladiator pummel each other with Pugil Sticks, each attempting to shove their opponent off within 30 seconds. Contenders earn 10 points for a victory; 5 points for remaining on the platform

ELIMINAT

After battling for points against the mighty Gladiators, contenders then undergo the final challenge known as ELIMINATOR.

They go head-to-head against one another, with the one who has accumulated the most points getting a headstart.

The agonising course is as follows:
* Over and under four hurdles
* Climb a rope
* The men pedal 6m (20 ft) while dangling from a hand bike. The women swing from rung to rung while dangling from a 6m (20 ft) ladder.
* Climb a cargo net
* Slide down a 28m (90 ft) zip-line
* Traverse a 10m (32 ft) balance beam
* Run up the travelator
* Swing on a rope to smash through the finishing 'gate'

Easy, it isn't!

The winner is the first contender to break through the finish. In the event of a tie the race is re-run after a rest period. In a re-run contenders start together.

OR

EQUIPMENT

Gladiators and contenders are required to wear safety equipment which varies from event to event. Among the armoury are gloves, neck braces, breast plates, ankle braces, gum shields, knee and elbow pads and hard or soft helmets.

FALCON

Off duty Falcon loves to read,
go to the cinema or go out walking – and she has
recently taken up climbing.
Her son, Adam, helps her to answer all
her fan-mail.

► FALCON FACTS ◄

BIRTHDATE:
6 NOVEMBER 1963

BIRTHPLACE:
BRIGHTON

STARSIGN:
SCORPIO

HEIGHT:
170CM (5' 7")

WEIGHT:
67KG (10ST 7LBS)

STATS:
91-66-89CM (36-26-35 INS)

Falcon has her good friend Jet to thank for her initial introduction to the Gladiators. "At the time the producers were looking for a new female Gladiator," she recalls. "They had seen lots of girls, but hadn't found the right one. Then Jet put my name forward and I was amazed to receive the call asking me to do the trials. The next day I learned that I was to be Falcon. I felt brilliant."

Since then high flying Falcon has become one of the most formidable of the female Gladiators and says she "wouldn't change it for the world!"

Her motto – "They shall not pass" – serves her well, particularly in Gauntlet, an event at which she really excels. She also likes Joust, Powerball, Hang Tough and Atlaspheres.

FASHANU

Ex-soccer star John Fashanu has been involved with Gladiators ever since the first series back in 1992. In fact, John and his lovely co-presenter Ulrika Jonsson are as much a part of the show as Trojan, Jet or any of the Gladiators themselves.
       The show just wouldn't be the same without them!

John was born in Kensington, in September 1962. His football career began as an apprentice with Norwich City, and he progressed quickly at Carrow road to become the club's youngest-ever first-team player.

He helped the Canaries to promotion into the First Division before moving on to Crystal Palace, Lincoln City and Millwall. Then in 1986 he joined up-and-coming Wimbledon for £125,000 Once again he was a major factor in a promotion push to the top flight. And in 1988 he played in the Dons' side which so famously beat Liverpool 1-0 in the FA Cup final at Wembley. He also played for England.

John's playing career ended with Aston Villa, following a series of injuries.

Throughout his career John had found time to help others and has been involved in a number of fund raising activities for the aged, for underprivileged children and he's been active in the fight against racism.

His television career has seen him appearing on such shows as You Bet! Surprise Surprise, Six O'Clock Live, ITV's Telethon, A Question of Sport and Wish You Were Here. John has also presented Seven Sport for Channel 4 and Good Sport for the BBC.

And, of course, he's always been a big hit in Gladiators!

FANS

Gladiators' just wouldn't be the same without the fans. They are just great - and they really enjoy themselves!

FITNESS

Amazon says: "I train everyday. Sometimes it can be just half an hour on an exercise bike, other days it can be a good two hour stint in the gym. It tends to vary, but I do at least four weight training sessions a week. "Gladiators' training is heavier than when I was swimming. The kind of training I did before was probably more geared to the cardiovascular side of things whereas nowadays, although I have to be fit for the show, none of the games are longer than a minute.

Nightshade says: "I love to do lots of stepping and aerobics to music. The music is very important - in fact, if the music isn't good, then the exercise isn't so good and I find I can't do it properly. "

GAUNTLET

G is for GAUNTLET, one of the most gruelling Gladiators' events. The Contender has to battle his or her way down a 45m (50yds) corridor which is guarded by no less than FIVE Gladiators! And there's a time limit of just 30 seconds. Scoring: 10 points for making it through gauntlet within 20 seconds; 5 points for completing the course in less than 30 seconds.

G-FORCE

G-Force are the troupe of super-fit and very glamourous Cheerleaders who entertain the fans between events!

HANG TOUGH

Twelve feet above the ground two contenders and two Gladiators swing from a grid of 60 rings placed 1.2m (4 ft) apart. The object for the contenders is to remain aloft and swing 15m (50 ft) across to the Gladiators' platform. Naturally the Gladiators aim to stop their progress and remove them from the rings. Ten points are awarded for a successful crossing; 5 points for remaining aloft in the scoring zone.

HIT AND RUN

A scary event in which the Contender attempts to cross a 7.3m (24 ft) bridge, 3.7m (12 ft) off the ground. Meanwhile the Gladiators try their best to knock the contender off the bridge by swinging huge demolition balls in their direction. Contenders earn 2 points for each successful crossing within a 1 minute time limit.

Even among the Gladiators themselves, Hunter is considered one of the fittest guys around. He is one of the most competitive too. and has become first-choice for Skytrak, is the fastest climber on the wall - and he's virtually unbeatable in Pole Axe.

▶ HUNTER FACTS

BIRTHDATE:
2 JUNE 1973

BIRTHPLACE:
BEVERLEY

STARSIGN:
GEMINI

HEIGHT:
191CM (6' 3")

WEIGHT:
114KG (18ST)

STATS:
CHEST 130CM (51"), WAIST 84CM (33"),
ARMS 48CM (19"), LEGS 71CM (28")

HUNTER

These days Hunter trains even harder than ever before and has changed his routine to make himself more 'athletic'.
He's certainly come a long way since winning the Junior North East Britain Body Building championship.
He was working as a printer at the time but the course of his future changed dramatically when Gladiators' producer Nigel Lythgoe spotted his picture in a body building publication.
The young printer was called in for a try-out and, within a few days, was the latest member of the Gladiators squad - fully equipped with a new name...Hunter!

I

INTERNATIONAL GLADIATORS

Each year a selection of British Gladiators and Contenders compete in International Gladiators tournament, which have been held in Birmingham and Australia.

A great favourite among Gladiators fans, the lovely Jet is also a very busy lady out of the arena – in fact, her diary is full to bursting!

JET FACTS

BIRTHDATE:
13 FEBRUARY 1970

BIRTHPLACE:
TEESIDE, CLEVELAND

STARSIGN:
AQUARIUS

HEIGHT:
167CM (5' 6")

WEIGHT:
58KG (9ST 5LBS)

STATS:
96-61-91CM (38-24-36INS)

JET...

Here are just a few of the projects Jet has been working on lately...

* Writing and presenting The Bodyworks for Tyne-Tees TV
* Appearing on Anglia's debate programme The Warehouse
* Travelling to Australia to take part in International Gladiators
* Co-presenting LWT's You Bet!
* Being a regular DJ on Newcastle's Metro FM radio station
* Making loads of personal appearances
* Speaking to youth audiences on Motivation and Self-esteem
* Appearing in Aladdin at the Cambridge Corn Exchange
* Making a fitness video for youngsters
...And, of course, she is always keeping fit for the most important show of them all – Gladiators!

JOUST

Gladiator and Contender, both armed with a combat club, sit astride twisting, turning and swerving sky bikes – and attempt to unseat their opponent within a minute. Unseating a Gladiator is rewarded with 10 points; 5 points are given for staying on the bike!!

K is for

KISSES...

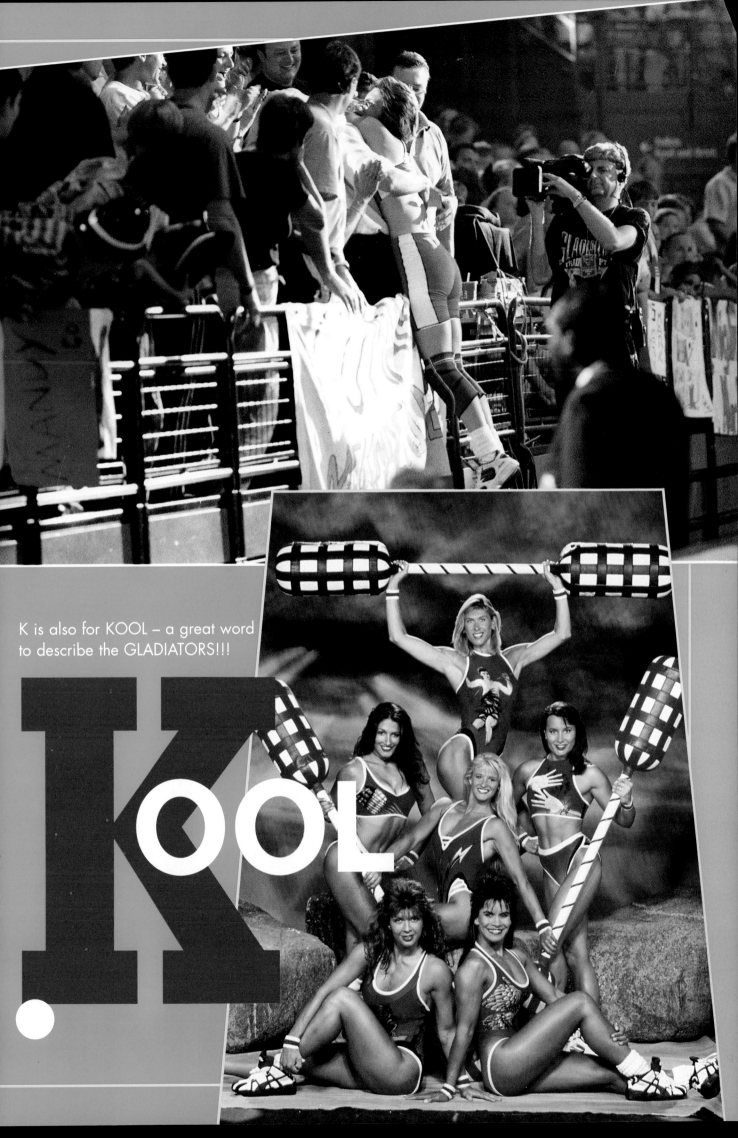

K is also for KOOL – a great word to describe the GLADIATORS!!!

KOOL

Lightning, the striking blonde Gladiator, is one of the most agile members of the team.

Lightning's combination of deadly determination, grace and femininity come from her background as a gymnast.

At the tender age of six she followed in her sister's footsteps and joined the gymnastics club where she would receive first class tuition and guidance for the next ten years. In that time she competed all over Great Britain as well as in Bulgaria, Belgium and Germany.

Her father was one of her coaches and later became her partner in weight training.
She has also competed in various Miss Figure Body Building tournaments, including the British Championship finals in which she was placed second.

◄ LIGHTNING FACTS ►

BIRTHDATE:
25 DECEMBER 1971

BIRTHPLACE:
BURNTWOOD, STAFFS

STARSIGN:
CAPRICORN

HEIGHT:
170 CM (5' 7")

WEIGHT:
59 KG (9ST 3LBS)

STATS:
96-66-89 CM (38-26-35 INS)

LIGHTNING

Lightning loves animals - she has a real soft spot for dogs, but also likes gorillas! Her hobbies include badminton, theatre and cinema-going and eating in good restaurants - but she really likes to devote her valuable spare time to her family

Lightning is currently concentrating on more cardiovascular workouts, increasing her fitness level and keeping her heart strong and healthy while sustaining low body fat. Five times a week she works out in her own gym at home – consisting of machines, free weights, bikes and steppers.

During the past few years Lightning has appeared in numerous TV shows and is keen to develop her talents as a presenter.

She enjoyed presenting the Gladiators' Train to Win, especially as she was able to pass on her experience to the youngsters in the show.

In the winter she just loves pantomime and has so far appeared in productions of Cinderella, Robin Hood, Babes in the Wood and Dick Whittington.

EAN MACHINE

In Gauntlet few contenders get past the MEAN MACHINE – the ultra cool combination of Warrior, Trojan, Saracen, Hunter and Rhino!

M is for MAGNIFICENT – and that's just what the GLADIATORS are!!!

MAGNIFI

USCLES

M is also for MUSCLES –
you see plenty of them in
GLADIATORS.

The latest series welcomes three new faces to the Gladiators squad. They are... RIO...REBEL...and ACE...

RIO

Former ambulance driver JANE GRACE OMOROGBE gave up her job after passing an initial Gladiators selection to put every effort into becoming part of the TV super-heroes team.

Having spent two months intensively training with former Olympic Tae kwon do coach Tony Slaney, she then competed, against 60 other hopefuls, in the rigorous fitness test.

Jane (25), has also modelled (bridal gowns for Geddes-Muir Designs) and last July won the title of Miss Wessex 1995 and was one of the finalists in the Miss United Kingdom beauty contest which was held in London last July.

Jane left school with nine GCSE's and three A levels and became an accounts clerk. She joined the Ambulance Service in 1991 and acquired advanced driving and first aid skills.

She stands at a physically intimidating 6'1" tall and weighs 12 stones. Her hobbies include Tae kwon do, portraits and sculpture, dancing and dress making along with circuit and weight training.

She says: "I have a great deal of respect for the Gladiators and really look forward to bringing my fitness talents to the team."

ACE

WARREN FURMAN wanted to shout it from the roof tops when he was offered the chance to become a Gladiator and he would have been in a perfect position to do so at this 23-year-old's day job as a roofer.

The producers of the hit TV show were impressed by a photograph of Warren and invited him along with 60 other hopefuls to an ardous audition and passed with flying colours.

W
ACES

"I was given only two weeks to prepare for the test but on the day I felt terrific and full of energy, I really enjoyed taking part and at the end the producer came over and shook me by the hand and gave his congratulations. I am sure I will be a great asset to the team as I'm strong but agile, fit and above all, focussed. Although I have great determination, I also enjoy having fun."

Warren, one of four brothers, left school at 16 and became an apprentice sign maker. He joined his father's roofing business before having a crack at modelling while also working as a newspaper printer. He admits he wasn't quite ready for the demorilising round of auditions necessary to get himself cast in commercials and gave it up in favour of concentrating on body-building. He now works as a roofer with his brother.

His hobbies are tennis, fitness training and boxing for fitness. Warren is six foot tall, and weighs 16 stones.

REBEL

Top international athlete JENNIFER ELAINE STOUTE is best known for her amazing Olympic, European and Commonwealth victories.

A runner with 1992 Olympic team, she was a semi finalist in the 200m and brought home the bronze in the 4x400m. She also took the bronze in the same event at the European Games in 1990 but was covered in glory at the Commonwealth Games that year when she won the gold in the 4x400m, the silver in the 4x100m and was a finalist in the 200 and 400m races.

Jennifer was also a finalist in the 1986 Commonwealth Games and the 1988 Olympics. All in all, a brilliant sporting background to join the Gladiator force.

Between her remarkable sporting achievements, Jennifer has worked as a clerical assistant in the Corporate Relations department of London Electricty. She is currently studying for a diploma in Marketing.

Her interests mainly revolve around sport but she also enjoys reading, life drawing and modelling.

"I'm not someone to mess around with," says Nightshade. "The contenders know I'll make 'em work for their prizes. Believe me, they know!"

NIGHTSHADE

And she loves making 'em work in the fast and furious events. In fact, the faster and more furious, the better! "My favourite event is Powerball - a full minute of running, diving and thinking on your feet. In fact, I like all the team events.

"Last year was the hardest I've had since I became a Gladiator. I caught a virus when I went to Australia for the Ashes. I was quite ill and seemed to have flu all the time. I got hurt and injured in a fall. But the show must go on, as they say, and the support I got from the other Gladiators was a tribute to the brilliant team-spirit that we have.

"When I got home I was still quite poorly, and two boys who live nearby knocked on my door and said they hadn't seen me out running, and they gave me this amazing pot plant to cheer me up. I don't have 'green fingers', but this plant is amazing. I don't even know who they are but I'd like to say a big 'thank you' to them. Their gesture showed how great the fans are. It's things like that which make being a Gladiator so nice."

Off duty Nightshade says she likes to do quiet things. "I like to read, listen to music – to watch TV or videos, to sew or just relax with my husband. And my friends will tell you I'm also a very good baby-sitter!

▶ NIGHTSHADE FACTS ◀

BIRTHDATE:
14 November 1960

BIRTHPLACE:
Kingston Town, Jamaica

STARSIGN:
Scorpio

HEIGHT:
183cm (6')

STATS:
91-66-91cm (36-26-36ins)

FAVOURITE EVENT:
Powerball

LEAST LIKED EVENT:
Swingshot

FAVOURITE FOOD:
West Indian 'lots of spices'

OUCH!

Being a Gladiator is a tough business, with plenty of knocks and bruises – and sometimes something more serious.

For instance, Zodiac recalls a collision in Powerball which knocked her unconscious. "I was very, very confused when I came round. I was concussed and afterwards the other Gladiators found me wandering in the hotel corridors!"

Panther fell during Tilt and suffered a back injury which kept her out of action for five long months.

Saracen injured himself by turning on his ankle and had to hobble around on crutches for a while. "I also had to retire from the Wall when I injured my ribs, and I had a fall in one of the international shows!"

Amazon met the 'Ouch factor' in her very first Gladiators season. "I had a cruciate ligament injury when I ended up at the bottom of a pile of bodies at the bottom of the Pyramid. It meant I missed out on the semi-finals, the finals and the international shows. Unfortunately injuries are an occupational hazard for the Gladiators!"

OVER THE TOP

PANTOS

Gladiators are in great demand each Christmas to appear in pantomimes all over the country.

POLE AXE

Gladiator and contender race up a 10.4m (34 ft) pole using struts protruding from the pole. First to the top strikes a button which causes the struts to retract and deposits the opponent back on the ground! Ten points are awarded to successful Contenders.

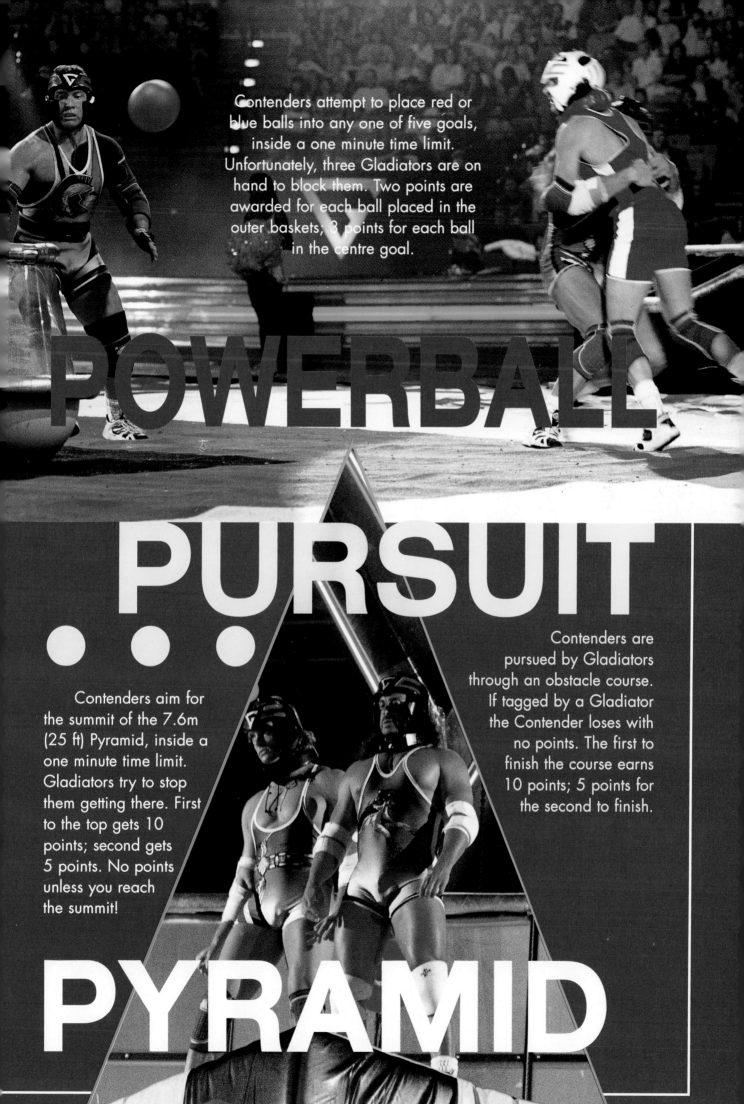

Contenders attempt to place red or blue balls into any one of five goals, inside a one minute time limit. Unfortunately, three Gladiators are on hand to block them. Two points are awarded for each ball placed in the outer baskets; 3 points for each ball in the centre goal.

POWERBALL

PURSUIT

• • •

Contenders aim for the summit of the 7.6m (25 ft) Pyramid, inside a one minute time limit. Gladiators try to stop them getting there. First to the top gets 10 points; second gets 5 points. No points unless you reach the summit!

Contenders are pursued by Gladiators through an obstacle course. If tagged by a Gladiator the Contender loses with no points. The first to finish the course earns 10 points; 5 points for the second to finish.

PYRAMID

PANTHER

As a youngster Panther and her brother were encouraged by their father to take up judo. "He was a 4th Dan Black Belt, and my brother and me both achieved Brown Belts," she says.

Panther is a mad keen soccer fan who supports Newcastle United. If Gladiators had alternative names, perhaps her's would be 'Magpie'!

► PANTHER FACTS ◄

BIRTHDATE:
14 OCTOBER 1963

BIRTHPLACE:
BLYTH

STARSIGN:
LIBRA

HEIGHT:
170 CM (5' 7")

WEIGHT:
66KG (10ST 7LBS)

STATS:
94-61-91 CM (37-24-36 INS)

On leaving school she became a clerk/typist and later a personal secretary grappling with facts and figures in a Chartered Accountancy firm. But it was her own figure that was to lead her on the road to fame when she took up body building in a big way.

Success came in the form of four amateur titles – Miss Britain, Miss Russia, Miss Europe and Miss Universe. However, her beginnings as a Gladiator could be described as a kind of Gotcha! in reverse. She was interviewed, while wearing a bikini, by none other than Noel Edmonds on TV. Watching the interview was producer Nigel Lythgoe, who was then preparing the first series of Gladiators.

Within days the glamourous body builder had undergone strenuous strength and stamina tests and soon afterwards she became Panther!

Being a Gladiator can sometimes be a funny experience. Panther recalls signing autographs for over an hour one day, when a very small boy walked up to her. "He was no more than six years-old – and he said 'Hello, Panther darling, any chance of a snog!' It was so funny."

QUIZ TIME

Can you answer these TEN Gladiators Questions? Turn to page 61 to see if you were right!

Turn to page 61 to see if you were right!

1 Which Gladiator was born in Bombay?
2 In which city is Gladiators recorded?
3 Which great rock band recorded the Gladiators' anthem 'Another One Bites The Dust'?
4 Which Gladiator was a world class swimmer?
5 Which Gladiator co-presents You Bet!?
6 Name the three Gladiators who are Tae Kwon Do experts.
7 Which Gladiator portrays Actionman on US TV?
8 Who is the fire fighting Gladiator?
9 How high is the Pyramid?
10 Which Gladiator loves to play golf?

RHINO FACTS

HEIGHT:
180 CM (5' 11")

WEIGHT:
114KG (18ST)

STATS:
CHEST 140CM (55"), WAIST 81CM (32")
THIGHS 74CM (29"), BICEPS 51CM (20")

FAVOURITE ACTORS:
DENZEL WASHINGTON,
ROBERT DE NIRO

He's thick-skinned, he's a tough as leather, he's incredibly fast and he can barge over any contender – he's Rhino!

Rhino joined Gladiators during the lives shows and graduated to the TV team for the last series. And he became an instant hit with the fans.

His awesome strength derives from his life as a former heavyweight body builder, at which he won many British Championships. He's been described as being 'as wide as he is tall'! and as having 'the power of a bull elephant'.

Away from the arena, Rhino likes collecting action videos and he has a great interest in conservation.

RHINO ● ● ● ●

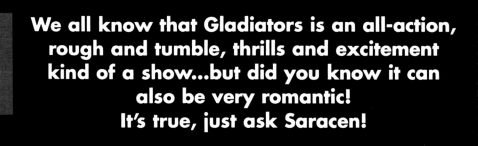

We all know that Gladiators is an all-action, rough and tumble, thrills and excitement kind of a show...but did you know it can also be very romantic! It's true, just ask Saracen!

SARACEN

The fire-fighting Gladiator actually met his future wife Chrissie during the recording of the first series in which she was a Contender - now they are happily married and living in south London.

Besides being a professional fire fighter, Saracen had quite a bit of on-screen experience before he became a Gladiator. Among other appearances he had been a 'double' for boxer Frank Bruno in a film about the great heavyweight.

These days, of course, he's a big star in his own right!

▶ SARACEN FACTS ◀

BIRTHDATE:
30 AUGUST 1963

BIRTHPLACE:
LONDON

STARSIGN:
VIRGO

HEIGHT:
193 CM (6' 4")

WEIGHT:
112KG (17ST 7LBS)

STATS:
CHEST 132 CM (52"), WAIST 86 CM (34"), BICEPS 51 CM (20")

SKY-TRAK

A scary event. Two Contenders, each tugging a detonator, are chased by two Gladiators while suspended upside-down on the Sky-Trak apparatus. The Gladiators attempt to strike the detonators to put the Contenders out of the event and without any points The first contender to finish gets 10 points: the second is awarded 5 points.

SUSPENSION BRIDGE

Armed with hammer heads Contender and Gladiator advance towards each other across the bridge. When they meet the action begins as they attempt to bundle one another into thin air. Contenders score 10 points if they manage to stay on the Suspension Bridge and remove the Gladiator; 5 points for a draw.

SWING-SHOT

Two Contenders, two Gladiators – all swinging on suspended shock cords. The Contenders aim to remove yellow, blue and red velcro scoring balls from a pole, then deposit them in a pod on his or her starting platform. Gladiators simply aim to stop them doing so. Scoring: 1 point for a yellow ball, 2 points for a blue ball, 3 points for a red ball. No points for an undeposited ball.

TILT

Gladiator and Contender are attached by a rope at the waist and stand opposite one another on tilt platforms. The Gladiator's platform is higher and angled forwards. In two 30-second pulls the Contender attempts to dislodge the Gladiator. Five points are awarded if the Gladiator leaves the platform. No points for a draw.

TROJAN FACTS

BIRTHDATE:
25 FEBRUARY 1968

BIRTHPLACE:
BASINGSTOKE

STARSIGN:
PISCES

HEIGHT:
188CM (6' 2")

WEIGHT:
102KG (16ST)

STATS:
CHEST 137CM (54") WAIST 81CM (32")
THIGHS 71CM (28") ARMS 51CM (20")

It's hard to believe that the handsome Trojan was once a shy, timid youngster. "But it's absolutely true," he confesses. "I was always nervous in front of girls and didn't have a girlfriend 'til I was seventeen."

TROJAN

It was an interest in body-building that was to bring him out of himself and build up his self-confidence. In fact, the sport took him from his home town of Basingstoke to Los Angeles where he began preparing to become a professional body builder.

Then came a trip back to England in 1993 and a try-out as a Gladiator in the second series. He became Trojan and has never looked back.

He always had an ambition to be an actor, and last year the dream came true when he was chosen to portray Action Man in a brand new 26 episode TV series shot in the USA.

But it is as Trojan the Gladiator that he is best loved in Britain. and he says he'll always be grateful to his fans. "It's been a fantastic time and I love meeting the fans — they mean a great deal to me."

TM

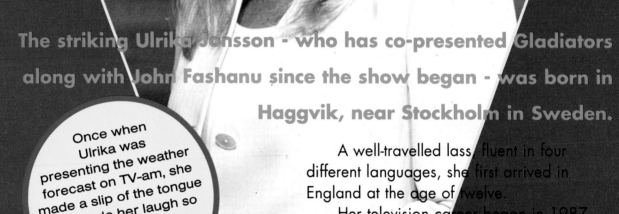

The striking Ulrika Jonsson - who has co-presented Gladiators along with John Fashanu since the show began - was born in Haggvik, near Stockholm in Sweden.

Once when Ulrika was presenting the weather forecast on TV-am, she made a slip of the tongue that made her laugh so much that she was unable to give the forecast!

A well-travelled lass, fluent in four different languages, she first arrived in England at the age of twelve.

Her television career began in 1987 when she became secretary to the managing director of TV-am. Within a year she had moved on and was appearing on-screen as a weather presenter for the Scandinavian satellite channel SCANSAT.

TV-am invited her back as their weather presenter - and she was soon a TV personality in her own right with many appearances to her name - including Growing Up Green, Backchat, Ulrika On The Move, Six O'Clock Live, Who's Bluffing Who, The Big Breakfast - and, of course, Gladiators!

ÜLRIKÄ

Ulrika has no desire whatsoever to take part in any of the Gladiators' events. "I'm much better at cheering others on!" she says. The tension and excitement is exhausting enough without having to rush around the arena being clobbered by Gladiators!"

VARIETY

The producers of GLADIATORS are always striving to include as much VARIETY in the show as possible!

VIEWERS

GLADIATORS is seen in Great Britain by an average audience of 14.5 million, making it one of the top-rated TV shows in the country.

VOGUE

● ● ● ●

Vogue is most definitely a lady in fashion. She's been a great hit since joining the Gladiators for the 1995 series, after a spell in the live shows.

Before that she had enjoyed life as a top-notch aerobics performer and was a member of a team that won the National Aerobic Championship and then became European Champions.

Landing her role in TV's toughest team marked the fulfilment of a great personal ambition for Vogue. "I've wanted to be a Gladiator ever since the show first started on TV," she says. "But my involvement in the Aerobics team meant that I just didn't have the time to put in the 100% training required for the try-out."

► **VOGUE FACTS** ◄

HEIGHT:
168CM (5' 6")

WEIGHT:
64KG (10ST)

CHEST:
97CM (38")

WAIST:
64CM (25")

TM

Vogue's 'try-out' for Gladiators proved to be one of the toughest tests that she had ever been through. "We had to walk the length of a school gymnasium on our hands while dragging a heavy tray with our feet. Then came thirty jumps on and off a plastic box, followed by a return journey with that tray. Next came ten circuits of the room before we finished with thirty rebound jumps over a four-foot high beam." Phew!!!

Warrior, the biggest of the Gladiators, is a fierce fighting machine in the arena, and a real gentle giant out of it.

Just watching him in action in events like Tilt and Powerball, you realise the awesome power and strength contained within that massive body. See him talking with young fans after a show and you know that he wouldn't harm a fly!

When he's off duty Warrior likes nothing better than a round of golf – he's a pretty good player with a five handicap. In his time, he has also been a footballer, a decathlete and a rugby player – an England Under-19s Colt, no less. And, before joining the Gladiators, he was training as a professional body builder.

Did You Know...Warrior appeared in an opera called The Empress and Facts which was shown on Channel 4!

WARRIOR

BIRTHDATE:
30 December 1960

BIRTHPLACE:
St Helens

STARSIGN:
Capricorn

HEIGHT:
196cm (6' 5")

WEIGHT:
132kg (20st 12lbs)

STATS:
Biceps 56cm (22"), Thighs 79cm (31"")
Waist 97cm (38"), Chest 142cm (56")

TM

WALL

The Wall is one of the most exciting Gladiators events. Male contenders are given a 10 seconds start over their Gladiator pursuers (females 15 seconds), as they scale the 10m (36ft) edifice. Five points are awarded if a contender remains on The Wall after 1 minute; 10 points for reaching the top!

The dictionary defines a wolf as a 'fierce wild animal' – and our own Wolf would not disagree with that!

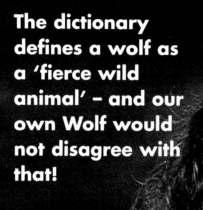

WOLF – A DAY IN THE LIFE

"Wake up at 7am, then eat breakfast before going to the arena at about 8.30. Start warming up for the events. Go to the first event. If the crowd is hostile towards me I'll have a go at them.

"After the show I'll go to the hospitality suite to meet some fans.

"There's a very short break and then we do another show, and again go to hospitality.

"Return to hotel around 11 pm. Have a nice long, hot bath and then try to get some sleep before doing the same things all over again next day!"

► WOLF FACTS ◄

BIRTHDATE:
30 SEPTEMBER 1952

BIRTHPLACE:
BOMBAY, INDIA

STARSIGN:
LIBRA

HEIGHT:
183CM (6' 0")

WEIGHT:
95KG (15ST)

STATS:
BICEPS 46CM (18") THIGHS 74CM (29")
WAIST 76CM (30") CHEST 122CM (48")

WOLF

The snarling Gladiator who's always getting into trouble really identifies with his now famous name. "Nobody is meaner or tougher than the Wolf-Man," he says.

He's even something of a 'lone wolf' when it comes to the events – brilliant in one-on-one situations, but sometimes a bit too 'individual' in the team games.

That just adds to the mystique of the 'Gladiator We Love to Hate'!

X- is for... XCITEMENT*

That's what you get in every GLADIATORS tournament!

*Okay, we know that's not the way to spell excitement. But can you think of anything beginning with 'X'???

Y is for YOU

Y is for YOU – the viewers. We thank you for watching, and for your support. Remember, without YOU there would be no GLADIATORS!

ZODIAC FACTS

BIRTHDATE:
2 November 1965

BIRTHPLACE:
London

STARSIGN:
Scorpio

HEIGHT:
175cm (5' 9")

WEIGHT:
62kg (9st 11lbs)

STATS:
97-64-89cm (38-25-35 ins)

™

ZODIAC

Heavenly Zodiac is among the most athletic of all the Gladiators. This is not surprising as she has been Great Britain's women's pole-vaulting champion since 1992, has broken many records and is listed at number 11 in the world rankings!

It was her athletics' coach Tom McNab who first suggested that she try-out for Gladiators in 1993. She applied, succeeded in the trials, was signed-up for the live shows at Wembley, and was given the name 'Zodiac'. Next came more trials – with Hunter – which led to a place in the team for the 1993 series. She says that being chosen from over 9,000 applicants really gave a great big boost to her confidence and self-esteem. Since then Zodiac hasn't looked back...and has become one of the most competitive Gladiators: "My competitive nature gives me an edge," she says. "I never give in!"

When she's off-duty Zodiac loves to go horse riding at dawn, take long walks in the park, swim or learn new sports. She says she also sleeps a lot!

We'll end as we began
– with some more great
pictures of the
Gladiators in action...

COMPETITION

WIN AN OFFICIAL GLADIATORS SWEATSHIRT!

All you have to do is answer these three simple questions:

1. Who won the men's tournament in Britain in series 4?

2. Who won the women's tournament in Britain in series 4?

3. In which country was Ulrika Jonsson born?

All the answers can be found in this Gladiators' Special.

Write your answers on a postcard or envelope with your name, age and address and send to:

**Gladiators Competition
Grandreams Limited
Jadwin House
205-211 Kentish Town Road
London NW5 2JU**

Closing date for entries is March 31st 1997.

The first three correct entries drawn out of the bag on the closing date will be awarded Gladiators sweatshirts. The publisher's decision is final and no correspondence will be entered into.

QUIZ ANSWERS

① **Wolf** ② **Birmingham** ③ **Queen** ④ **Amazon** ⑤ **Jet** ⑥ **Nightshade, Rio and Raider** ⑦ **Trojan** ⑧ **Saracen** ⑨ **7.6 metres** ⑩ **Warrior.**